the family at home

anita kaushal

with photographs by penny wincer

the family at
home

LOVE. LIFE. STYLE.

CLARKSON POTTER / PUBLISHERS
New York

contents

start

home

is a word that resonates deeply. For many people it evokes family, childhood, some of their most vivid memories. It is a word that conjures images and emotions. If we're lucky, it is a word that brings comfort to the soul, that names a place we want to return to, that makes us feel safe, loved and nurtured. We may not all have grown up in the ideal environment, but we can relate to the hope of inspiring these feelings in our own home. In this book, I explore what 'home' means to us as individuals and as families, how we choose to arrange and decorate our living spaces and, more importantly, the way we choose to live in them. Our home-life can have a huge impact on who we are; as adults it affects our daily lives and moods, and for children it influences the kind of people they will become.

There have been countless books on raising children and on decorating, but here I consider both together. It is a kind of manual or recipe book, a collection of ideas based on the heartfelt philosophy that it is possible to create a home that is both beautiful and nurturing. Embracing the modern concept that children are a natural part of our lives, neither inconvenient beings nor precious centres of the universe, this book focuses on the needs of both parent and child as a unified whole.

The true enjoyment of a home is as much about the things that we do there – sleeping, eating together, conversing, sharing books and yes, even watching television – as it is about what we put into it. Truly improving our home environment means enhancing those familiar routines and rituals, while making it easy for parents and children to play and create together. Sometimes you can do this by simply using what you already have in a better way, or by adding small things to get the balance right.

The book is divided into four themes, each concentrating on the spaces in a home and the activities that take place in each. We begin with 'Live', which offers examples and ideas for making the living areas of a home stylish as well as adaptable to the needs of children and adults.

'Share' looks at the kitchen and dining areas, where we come together to cook, eat and celebrate with family and friends. 'Nest' is about calm, restful spaces, such as bedrooms and bathrooms, where we relax, sleep and retreat from the outside world. 'Bare' brings in light and air, with suggestions on gardening together, nature discovery and caring for the planet. Throughout these chapters are practical ideas and inspirations taken from the homes that are featured in the book. Finally, 'Find' is a reference tool that lists further information on the products, suppliers and manufacturers of some of the items shown.

Going beyond the purely aesthetic, *The Family at Home* offers a collection of some of the best ideas I have seen for making the home a stylish and welcoming environment while responding to our family's daily rhythms. Although beautifully photographed, these are real houses inhabited by real people with children. And while I have shared a number of decorating tips and listed some of the best resources I have found, the book is not meant to be a 'how to', but rather a source of inspiration, a scrapbook, if you will, of sparkling examples to be considered, adapted or merely appreciated as you create your own ideal of home.

Look to your children for clues...

When thinking about what we want from our HOMES and how we want to live in them, there can be no better starting point than looking to our children. Their HONESTY, strength of conviction and confidence could do much to TEACH us about how we might live. Confronting the practical NECESSITIES of a child-inclusive home can help us to be more *realistic* about styles and trends we may have imposed on ourselves, without ever questioning whether they really suited our *personality* and LIFESTYLE. Living in a home that is true to our sense of VALUES helps us to rediscover a life that resonates with our children and feels *comfortable* to us.

live

Live, work and play. Rooms for all reasons. We play with our children and leave them to play on their own, listening to them and enjoying time together in silence. Our home is the one place that accommodates the needs, wants and desires of the many different personalities that live in it.

Compromise is the key in living areas, as no matter how lovely your children's bedrooms, they will want to drag favourite toys to the place where you are. So relax and enjoy the Sunday papers on the sofa, knowing that Teddy and his friends will be sat beside you. Develop a new skill in tiptoeing through the building blocks while balancing a magazine and a hot cup of coffee, and realize that the remote control will never be where you left it. Do all of these things safe in the knowledge that when the time comes, the toys can be put away and the room can return to being the calm place in which you relax with friends and family. Of course, you may want to have a room that is simply off-limits to children and their many apparatus. But this may pose practical issues of its own, not to mention lots of admonitions. I don't believe in hiding precious pieces that give comfort and personalize a home. After all, communal spaces are there to be enjoyed by everyone. Indulge your senses and appreciate all those things that give your home its soul, but do so on the understanding that things can get broken. The chances are if you relax and enjoy your living space, your children will, too. It's not so much about what you have in your home, but more your attitude to it. There are many ingredients that go together to make a space work, with or without children. Colour, pattern, texture and lighting add to the interest, warmth and comfort, and ultimately determine the mood of a room. By introducing elements of your child's personality through artwork and elevating its status with beautiful frames, you give your wall space colour and your child confidence. And by decorating in a way that appeals to you, creating a home that is true to yourself and your family, it will be all the more appealing to your children.

welcome

What a feeling of relief, when you return after a long day, a tiring journey, or just a taxing visit to the grocery store. You turn the key and enter, kick off your shoes, put down your bags, school folders and shopping, and feel the welcome of your own home. The hallway is a utilitarian space, but signals home and gives a sense of those that inhabit it. More than just a traffic corridor, the entrance hall is an opportunity to display photos and objects that say 'welcome home'. What does your hallway say about you? Is it inviting to others, or even to you?

show Photographs personalize a home and make good use of a vast expanse of wall. They remind us of the value of our past and the possibilities that lie in our future. Give photos an old-fashioned feel by having an entire selection reprinted in sepia or black and white, or group a series together by colour, subject or mood. Before hanging a collection, make paper templates and play with these on the wall to see how they work together.

Opposite: The geometric tiles in the hallway of this period house make a fitting backdrop to the modern chair, a design by Harry Bertoia. Previous page: An antique French armchair sits opposite stools from Ikea. Light pours through the hall, which is kept clear of large furnishings for better flow and easy tidying.

A hall is what makes sense of your life. This little niche in the hallway holds both precious and everyday objects, as everyone should have a place to lay their keys and pick up a little inspiration at the same time. The floral wallpaper adds a jewel-box feel to the tableau. Opposite: A massively enlarged photograph adds life to a hall corner. The chair makes the hallway feel more part of the living space instead of just a transit area.

'Real isn't how you are **MADE**', said the Skin Horse. 'When a child *loves* you for a **long, long** time, not just to *play* with, but REALLY loves you, then you become Real.'

Margery Williams, *The Velveteen Rabbit*

cherish childhood memories

light The way we use light is as much a decorative statement as any wallpaper or piece of furniture, and affects the mood of a room and the people in it. Gone are the days of the single pendant glaring from the middle of the ceiling. Light should be at different intensities for different activities, and can create a sense of excitement, relaxation or focus. Be sure to have some softer mood lighting, perhaps in the form of candles, an indulgence to save for when the children are asleep.

The string of paper lanterns consists of cubes that have all been individually painted to make a cheerful, glowing light and varying patterns. Opposite: A perfect example of form and function, this giant alphabet puzzle allows children to control the mood lighting of a room simply by adding and taking away the pieces. Overleaf: An airy hallway features an illuminated growth chart.

lounge

A dictionary definition reads 'to pass time lazily or idly', and this is something we should all be able to do well in our own home. As satisfying as it is to make rooms tidy and beautiful, we all need our portion of comfort: a soft chair or sofa (and if we can jump on it, so much the better), cushions on the floor, or a really squishy rug that we can lie on to do puzzles or read the paper by the fire. Everyone has their own idea of the perfect place for doing nothing, and whether your living space is modern, traditional, open-plan or intimate, it should be one that invites you to switch off and just be.

pattern A room need not be filled with bright primary colours to be attractive to children. Splashes of colour and a mix of texture and pattern can combine to create a comfortable, inviting living space. Patterns don't have to match, in fact, the more clashing the better. The key to working with patterns is to layer. Fill the room only with pieces that please and excite, and regardless of what anyone else thinks, just do it with confidence and with your heart.

In this room, neutral colours on the walls, floor and sofa leave plenty of space for indulging in colourfully patterned accents in the rug, cushions and paintings. The bright lampshade at the right of the photograph was made by adding adhesive acetate to a plain shade. The Arco floor lamp is an Achille Castiglione design, rug by The Rug Company, child's table and stool by Ikea.

A conservatory space and hallway are made even brighter with
bold wall coverings and patterned chair cushions. Turn-of-the-century
chandeliers and geometric tiles lend an Old World style while the
wallpaper by Marianne Cotterill and plaster-of-Paris 'branch'
sculptures inject modern verve. The antique frame by Bycamera
looks stunning left empty and emphasizes the distinctive design
of the wallpaper.

Colour can have a *magical* effect on a house or room. As children we are INSTINCTIVELY drawn to the **bright** hues of rainbows, kaleidoscopes, even sweet wrappers. But as we grow older, too often our urge for something **bold** is dampened by what we *think* is acceptable. *Rediscover* your own taste for colour, and then have the **CONFIDENCE** to use it, whether in whole rooms or in *vivid* accents: stripes or patterns, floral or **GEOMETRIC**, bright or brighter?

colour
magic of a rainbow

open 'Open-plan' is the watchword for modern living. But lest it become a cliché, consider how family life flows naturally, and sometimes unstoppably, from kitchen to dining room to living room, and back the other way. Openness is about togetherness, about security, as children know you are around to listen. When people think open-plan, they often envision cold, static spaces, but these areas can be fun and creative. You can maintain a sense of order by grouping furnishings and storage sensibly and by creating cozy corners for quiet moments.

In this architect-designed house, a children's study area and playroom is reached by a 'fireman's pole' that drops down from the children's bedroom on the mezzanine level. The lower level is divided into spaces for play and for study. Built-in shelves make maximum use of space for books, display objects and toys. A conventional stair leads up to the bedrooms.

In this period house, wood floors add a solid, homely character to an otherwise modern interior, while the use of white opens up the room and reflects the light. Splashes of colour come alive against the other neutral tones. Areas for eating, sitting and reading are clearly defined without the need for walls or partitions. Ample storage for books and magazines and a choice of simple furnishings keep the small room feeling spacious. Sofa by Ronan and Erwan Bouroullec for Cappellini.

In the reading corner, an old library trolley is used to hold and display books and to move them round the room. The child's rocker was rescued from a skip and re-conditioned. Overleaf: An open-plan living area is made more inviting with a generous supply of large floor cushions upholstered in soft, bold fabrics. The wood-panelled wall also adds warmth to the space. All furnishings from Maison de Vacances, designed by Emmanuelle Fouks and Nicolas Mauriac.

A house filled with **music** is never dull or dispirited. Not everyone has space for a piano, but every home has room for music of some kind. From *singing* and LISTENING together to learning instruments, musical *experiences* aid children's development in a number of ways. Children love to **dance** and thrill to a *twirl* with mum and dad. You'll *wonder* why you don't do it more often.

music a universal language

play

Lest we forget, living spaces are for living and for playing, jumping, rolling about. The Victorians may not have let their children run through the house, but it's hard to see how they could have stopped it. While no one would suggest that your house should become a playground, it should be a space where you (and your children) can enjoy yourselves and, dare I say, have fun. Some areas will naturally be off-limits to boisterous activity, but the better equipped your house is to deal with the occasional romps, the more relaxed you will all feel.

absorb Play won't always happen in a separate room. Sometimes it will be a bedroom or a space used for other functions as well, such as television or computer. The idea is to locate space for playthings so that you and your children know where they belong and where the centre for their playtime should be. Then your attention to storage and display can be focused and more useful. And when the toys migrate, everyone knows where they ought to return.

This shared space allows for the meeting of two separate personalities, with the partitions creating two bedrooms and a joint play area. The cushioned cubbyholes allow the space to flow and the children can still 'visit' and communicate freely. They also make great nesting spots. Previous page: This house features a slide made of moulded Corian, which provides a more exciting alternative to stairs. Of course, the children aren't the only ones who take the easy way down. A well-placed beanbag at the bottom of the slide ensures a soft landing.

TIDY

Children's toys and accessories don't always have to end up in bright plastic boxes or specially designed trunks • Try using woven boxes, baskets and large bowls that you find pleasing but that can also take a little rough treatment • Especially in public areas, you might use more decorative pieces that are nice to look at and make great hiding places for clutter • Storage bowls below by Créa Créa.

STOW

Whether it's an architect-designed built-in, such as this one below by Michaelis/Boyd, or a sturdy shelving unit with drawers and cupboards, you can answer your need for more storage and for creating designated spaces by using a storage unit as a room divider • If it's a freestanding piece of furniture, be sure it is safe from tipping and that the floor joists are up to the weight of the piece when filled with books and toys.

store

playtime

EARLY DEVELOPMENT

Large kitchen utensils such as mixing spoons, whisks, turkey basters and rolling pins are perennial favourites • Rolling and squeezing dough is a wonderful sensory experience for children and also helps to strengthen hands and arms • From eighteen months a child plays happily with a bowl of water and a sponge • From the age of two, children will want to use other objects and experiment with materials in water • After the age of three children can begin to use cookie cutters.

TOP TOYS

Building blocks (and fitted plastic blocks, such as Lego) • Picture jigsaws and wooden puzzles with knobs for smaller children • Cars, planes and trains • Baby dolls with clothes and accessories • Doll's houses • Washable paints and crayons (with brushes and sponges) • Musical instruments • Craft box with pieces of coloured felt, straws, pipe-cleaners, buttons, glitter and other trimmings for sticking on paper with non-toxic glue • Zoo and farm animals • Tea set.

Whenever possible, try to invest in pieces that can be treasured by your children as they grow up, while at the same time are still appealing to adults. A vibrant needlepoint wall-hanging by Paul Smith for The Rug Company makes a wonderful complement to the children's own artwork. The long, wooden table by Jacqueline Morabito is fantastic for multiple tasks. The orange seat and wire chair are designs by Arne Jacobsen and Harry Bertoia.

hide It may be the modern way of living that makes us so concerned with storing things. Or maybe we just have a lot of stuff. Or maybe it's the fact that we no longer seem satisfied with large, bulky cupboards and look for more creative solutions to storage. Organizing toys, books, games, clothes, dolls and precious objects is no mean feat. So it's worth having a look at all the options before giving up hope. Sometimes the answer is a lot simpler (and less expensive) than you might think.

A tepee provides a secret hiding place, somewhere to sneak off to, perhaps with a purloined snack. It is also a perfect place to hide toys. Transparent jars make ideal storage for smaller objects. Children can easily see what is inside without tipping it all out. The spiral tells a classic story and makes for an intriguing design above a fireplace. To make the spiral, see page 141. Opposite: A pretty screen does double-duty by camouflaging toy-filled baskets in the corner.

conceal It seems you can never have too much storage, especially
with children in the house. While it's lovely to display precious
pieces, it's also a good idea to keep the majority of toys and games
behind closed doors so children can take out one thing at a time.
It is far easier for children to focus and get enjoyment through play
when they are not bombarded with too much on show. Cupboards
are an obvious choice, but make sure they're sturdy. And if they
can also function as display spaces, so much the better.

toys They may want the much-hyped toy of the moment, but time and time again they will return to the basics that we, too, loved as children. There are some things video games can't replace, like the cuddly feel of a soft toy, the satisfying click of making a king in draughts, and the wonder of creating a painting of whatever their imagination desires, just with a few brush strokes.

Carved wood Noah's Ark figures are a traditional favourite. Opposite: The Beano wallpaper denotes a child's play area. Puzzles, paints, soldiers and dinosaurs are among the most popular toys that will never be out of fashion.

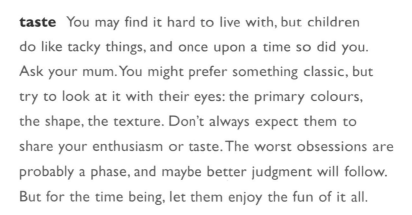

taste You may find it hard to live with, but children do like tacky things, and once upon a time so did you. Ask your mum. You might prefer something classic, but try to look at it with their eyes: the primary colours, the shape, the texture. Don't always expect them to share your enthusiasm or taste. The worst obsessions are probably a phase, and maybe better judgment will follow. But for the time being, let them enjoy the fun of it all.

Plastic ponies give a print by Helen Chadwick a whole new meaning. Today's popular toy may be tomorrow's collector's item, such as these early versions, so be careful what you throw out.

This, too, shall pass.

draw When we say children should be allowed to be creative, we aren't merely giving permission to draw on the walls, but to think outside the box. Art is as much about sharing ideas as it is about putting them on paper. Children who are encouraged when they think creatively will build confidence in their own ideas and sense of self. Language is creative, too. Talking to children about the art you look at together or about the things you see every day will enhance their visual awareness and sharpen their perception. When they do create their masterpiece, it deserves some wall space.

A well-stocked art drawer is one way to encourage creativity. Blackboard paint is an easy way to make a blank wall or cupboard into a space for expression. Toys that inspire are those that look and feel wonderful, such as this little girl's butterfly wings from a theatrical shop.

paint Children feel valued when they're allowed to
make their own mark and to contribute to their
surroundings. Having their drawings, paintings and other
creations around the house means the house is theirs,
too. And children's artwork adds so much colour and life,
not to mention unique design elements, to a room.
 A child's portrait reminds us of a moment in time and
can turn a dull corner into a space that makes you smile.

HARRY POTTER

Creating art projects together is a brilliant activity to share with your children. They may do painting at school or in art class, but they can easily get in touch with their creative side at home as well, and it may inspire you to do the same. This portrait was done by using an overhead projector to draw the outline and then applying thick paint with a spatula to get a textured effect. You could do the same with photographs or any scene that you'd like to recreate, or even project the image straight onto the wall to make a wall design.

BEST TOY

What better way to hold onto your child's best-loved toy than to immortalize it in a work of art? By the time it is banished to the bottom drawer, it may be battered and torn from being held so dear. Keep it fresh and preserve a sweet memory by having a portrait painted of the bedtime buddy, such as this one by Nell Johnson, or do it yourself, to keep or pass on to the grandchildren.

portrait

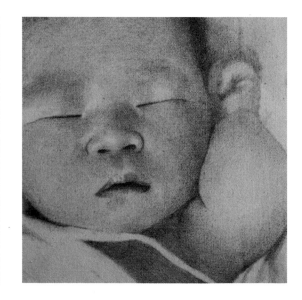

MUMMY

Children love to experiment with colour in art, and their particular vision of the world is priceless. Keep the best examples covered with a plastic or glass frame to preserve the freshness and protect these delicate mementoes. Once they have created their masterpiece, help them and the family to appreciate it by giving it a prominent position on their bedroom wall or elsewhere in the house.

PHOTOGRAPHY

Lots of photographs dotted around the house is a perfect way of recording and preserving the fleeting moments of child-hood. They can be casual snapshots, capturing family picnics or school outings, or more formal portraits to record a mile-stone event. There are many ways to display your memories, from sculptural surrounds to photo mobiles hung from the ceiling to good old-fashioned picture frames. When hanging photos on the wall, a good rule of thumb is to hang them two inches apart and to give your picture wall a theme.

PAINTING

Photographs are wonderful keepsakes, but a painted portrait of your child is a priceless work of art. Make sure you're familiar with the artist's work and that he or she has an understanding of your child's personality and, if possible, their favourite toys or activities in order to get a work that is most resonant of their individuality. This little girl's portrait is by Claerwen James. Opposite: A baby portrait in charcoal by Olivier Raab.

make Whether it's a designated room, an empty garage or a garden terrace, a place for big messy projects is enormous fun. It gives children space to expand their minds, their ambitions and their brush strokes. It's hard to bring up a budding Picasso if you're constantly cringing at the mess. So try to relax a little and use drop cloths if necessary.

The animals above are good examples of crafted objects for children to learn from. A plan chest and kitchen trolley provide easy-to-use storage for treasured artworks and supplies. Opposite: A giant papier-mâché shark is a long-term work-in-progress that the children can return to when the mood suits.

share

Sharing happens all around the house in many different ways, but the kitchen, the traditional hearth, is the real centre; the sharing of food is a life-affirming instinct. What more potent symbol of our sharing and nurturing can there be than communal mealtimes? What better way is there to connect and communicate with the people we value the most?

We give so much of ourselves outside the home (to work, study and daily commitments) that we sometimes have little energy for our nearest and dearest. But we all need to feel nourished and loved at home before we can offer ourselves to the wider world. Our kitchens are where we feed our families and where they come to be cared for. Kitchens and dining rooms are hives of activity, cooking, serving, talking, even homework at the table. They need to be robust and versatile spaces that adapt from mealtimes to conversation areas, from chef's domain to gathering place, welcoming and well organized, and, of course, child-friendly. A kitchen ought to be as much a child's domain as a parent's; it's where they gravitate because of the activity and because it's a place that engages their senses. In the kitchen, children become immersed in the sight, sound, smell, feel and taste of cooking. Sharing is about making the space easy and comfortable for everyone. It means having some things in the kitchen that are actually geared toward small children, special drawers they can play in, at least one cupboard that isn't off-limits and perhaps filled with those large, child-safe kitchen utensils that put so many designer toys to shame. It is preparing and cooking meals and treats with children, helping them learn about food, nutrition and the rewards of making something really wonderful with their own hands. And what more affectionate gesture to friends than to offer food prepared especially for them? My mother instilled in me the belief that cooking for others and entertaining is a privilege and that every grain of rice had someone's name on it. The idea was not to make it a huge challenge but a gift that we are happy to present because it benefits all.

cook

When we cook for others we give of ourselves. We can also be creative and experimental, cooking from old family recipes or inventing new ones from our own favourite foods and cookbooks. What we cook and how we approach food is part of our personal heritage and a wonderful way to pass on traditions to our children. Cooking is an activity that can be educational and bring us closer. Even when they're not helping, children are aware of the activity in the kitchen. If they are allowed to take part at times, they become more appreciative of what comes out.

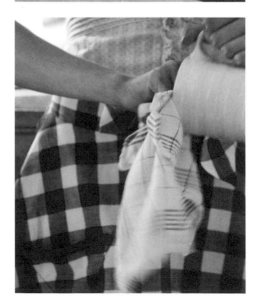

help From a very early age, children want to help. Toddlers love pulling a broom around or handing you plates from the dishwasher. The more ways you can let them help around the kitchen, the better they will understand the value of cooking and eating together. From playing with the mixing bowls early on to breaking eggs, pouring ingredients, rolling dough and cutting cookies by around the age of three, there are all kinds of ways children can help and, more importantly, be made to feel helpful. And there's no better way to get children to try food than to let them join in the making of it.

CHOCOLATE CHIP COOKIES
(makes 16–20)

100g (3½oz) butter, softened
60g (2oz) soft light brown sugar
1 egg, beaten
150g (5oz) plain flour
¼ tsp baking powder
few drops vanilla essence
100g (3½oz) good-quality chocolate, chopped

Preheat oven to 180°C/350°F/Gas 4. Cream together butter and sugar using a spoon or whisk, add the beaten egg. Fold in flour, baking powder, vanilla extract and chocolate pieces. Stir until combined, batter should be thick. Using a teaspoon, drop batter in lumps onto a greased cookie sheet. Bake for 8–10 minutes.

easy Organized doesn't mean perfect, but rather easy to access. In the kitchen, it means a space that puts parents and children at ease. There will always be the hazards of hot pots and ovens, but a kitchen will attract children and others, so the better it works for you, the more relaxed you will all be. Choose methods of storage and display that best suit the way you cook and serve, and your kitchen will be a happier place.

*Keeping books, crockery and food on display within reach
might seem rather precarious, but it serves to make older
children independent and comfortable in their environment.
The professional-style flexible tap is ideal for big clean-ups.
Low-level shelves can store books and unbreakables when
small children are in the house and more precious objects
when they are older. A tall metal catering trolley provides
lots of moveable storage. Previous pages: A rustic-style
kitchen offers all the necessities within easy reach and is
still orderly and pleasant.*

Every *grain*

of rice has someone's

NAME on it.

A clean, modern kitchen space is still user-friendly with open shelves that children can reach, large storage drawers and lots of natural light. Having ingredients such as herbs and spices on display makes a kitchen feel lived in without being cluttered.

bright Use splashes of colour in jars and crockery to give a taste of your own personality in the kitchen and dining area. If you are a fan of white walls and china, use accents to create vivid contrast with the simple elegance of your background. Or make the kitchen a collection of well-loved objects and cherished hand-me-downs.

This compact kitchen was purposefully given a bold treatment to define the space. The merry spice tins are family heirlooms and continue the bright hues of the vinyl gloss walls and upper units. The children's cups and plates are kept at low level and make their own colourful contribution to the overall palette. The sink is recycled catering supply, versatile and hardwearing.

We yearn to simplify our lives and yet feel the **need** to accumulate more. Our children learn by example how much is too *much* or never quite ENOUGH. A *few* well-chosen kitchen objects used creatively is surely better than a home full of *unnecessary* gadgets and extraneous toys. Give your children a cupboard of their own in the kitchen and fill it with *everyday* objects as toys. These TIMELESS playthings will not only improve your child's development, but fewer toys also make for better concentration.

less

everyday objects as toys

eat

These days we worry a lot about food: good food, bad food. Fortunately most of us do not have to worry about having enough to eat. So why not stop worrying so much and start enjoying? As long as you have a good variety of the basic food groups in your diet, and healthy snacks available around the kitchen, your family will eat well and happily. Children won't pine for artificially enhanced junk food if it isn't on display or kept enticingly out of reach. And if your own attitude to eating is positive and encouraging, it will go a long way toward leading them in the right direction.

good We all know what is meant by 'comfort foods'. There's a reason these are always basic, never too fussy and happily filling. Good food doesn't need fancy dress to be delicious, just good ingredients. Going back to basics is a start. Dust off those old recipes your mother (or your father) used to make and try allowing children to choose the dinner menu once in a while, letting them see how it's made so they can pass it on, too.

PERFECT SUNDAY LUNCH

• Get all of the family involved and head down to the shops for the newspapers.
• Pool out sections of the papers and sit down to chunky bread from the market with plenty of coffee for the grown-ups and freshly squeezed orange juice for the children.
• Serve the food in large dishes that children can help pass around.
• Favourite Sunday roasts include beef and Yorkshire pudding, pork with sage and onion stuffing and applesauce, lamb with mint sauce, chicken with roast potatoes, Cumberland sausages, bacon and eggs.
• Good vegetables to try are mashed swede, turnips, boiled cabbage, roast parsnips, carrots and peas. Favourite roasting potatoes include King Edward and Maris Piper varieties.

We take them for granted, but children *instinctively* use all their senses to get the most out of every experience. And we might be too quick to stifle EXPLORATION. Touching food is a natural way for young children to *understand* what they're eating and makes it more pleasurable for them. Even as adults we can appreciate the *delights* of engaging our senses. Who would eat popcorn with a spoon?

senses   live more fully

PACKED LUNCHES

Let children help choose what goes in • Use good containers that keep lunches from getting squashed • Lunches should include a protein (meat, fish, eggs, cheese, beans), a starch (bread, potatoes, rice or pasta) and at least one portion of veg and one of fruit • Use.granary or wholemeal bread for sandwiches • Peanut butter (and banana) • Chicken and lettuce • Cheese and pickle • BLT • Tuna and tomato • Salmon and cucumber • Hummus and lettuce.

WATER

It is such a source of good things and is vitally important to health and wellbeing. Water makes up 70 per cent of our body mass, and we all need to drink plenty to keep ourselves feeling well. Lack of water doesn't just make you feel thirsty, it can lead to listlessness, fatigue, irritability, problems with concentration, and headaches from dehydration. We can get water from food and other beverages, but children should be encouraged to drink water rather than juice or other drinks, especially after sports and play.

fuel

DAILY BREAD

Bread doesn't have to be boring. We all know that wholemeal is better than white, but try different varieties, shapes and sizes. Mixed-grain breads are good, too, and have a much more interesting flavour than white. Some children who don't like wholemeal on sandwiches do like it as buttered toast, especially if it's dripping with a little bit of honey. Seed breads have a lovely crunchy texture, especially when toasted. For sandwiches, try buns and rolls as well as flatbreads and wraps.

FOOD IS FUN

Feel the textures of foods, let them peel apples, shell peas, cut a tomato and count the seeds. Let them dig in and get messy. Food is fun! • Carrot sticks • Cheese chunks, alone or with ham slices, cherry tomatoes, cucumber slices or crackers • Celery sticks with peanut butter • Fresh fruit, sliced up for easier eating or for dipping in naturally sweetened yoghurt • Dried fruits and granola • Cereal bars.

GOOD FOR YOU

Milk, cheese, yoghurt, soya beans, tofu and nuts are rich in calcium • Red meat, liver, fish, pulses, green vegetables and fortified cereals for iron • At least two portions of fish a week for protein, vitamins and minerals • Milk, margarine, butter, green vegetables, carrots and apricots are all good sources of vitamin A • Citrus fruits, tomatoes and potatoes for vitamin C • Limit sweets to one day a week • Offer fruit instead of juice for less sugar and more nutrients • Vitamin A for eyes, B for muscles, C for healing, D for bones, E for skin.

delicious Healthy food can be tasty food, and children should learn that what's good for them is also wonderful to eat. A trip to the local farmers' market could be an eye-opening experience for the whole family, where children can choose (and taste) fruits and vegetables that have been allowed to ripen naturally. Freshly baked bread is almost a meal in itself. Providing good food for your family should be enjoyable, but don't forget the treats. We all need a little indulgence now and then.

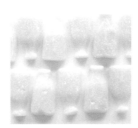

teatime Snacking is not a sin. Especially after school, when most children are ravenous from a day's playing and learning, offer them something rather than waiting for them to moan. Then you can make sure it's at least somewhat nutritious. Having teatime together gives you a chance to sit down with your children and talk about the day's happenings, over a cup of your favourite brew or a cool lemonade. Don't forget the biscuits!

HOME-MADE LEMONADE

Juice of 7 or 8 large lemons
½ cup of caster sugar (to taste)
5 cups cold water
1 large lemon, cut into small wedges

Combine in a large pitcher, stir to dissolve the sugar, and serve in tall glasses over ice.

The cottagey feel of this kitchen eating area is enhanced with a rustic wood table, built-in window seat and flagstone flooring. Other creative touches include a hand-crafted chandelier and retro-style fabrics on the windows and lampshade.

gather

Sitting together around the table is a simple yet fundamental family ritual. This is where we gather and converse, it may be the one place where we see each other at all. Eating breakfast together gives us time to bolster each other for the day ahead, at dinner we reconvene to share thoughts and experiences. The passing of food, plates and cutlery gives children the opportunity to help each other and to join in the community of family. Being engaged in mealtimes is about more than just refuelling our bodies, it develops our children's social skills and reinforces basic feelings of love, the joy of giving, of kindness and manners.

table Of all the major things that happen in your home, many will be centred round the dinner table. It's where children try their first solid food, learn to use a fork, do their homework, discuss friends and exam results. It's where arguments happen and reconciliation occurs, where laughter travels round like an electric current. It's where birthday cakes are lit and Christmas dinners are laid out. It's where memories are made and retold.

This kitchen and dining area in a converted Victorian schoolhouse takes advantage of ceiling height to separate the cooking area by setting it on a raised base. Built-in storage beneath and large cupboards provide plenty of room, and an enormous work surface is a cook's dream. The Ironbark table from Australia and axe-hewn teak benches from Bali make a homely contrast with the glossy resin floor and modern white surfaces of the Boffi kitchen units. Previous page: An eclectic mix of contemporary and traditional against a neutral and soothing background provides a suitable accompaniment to mealtimes. The chandelier from Grand Illusions has been personalized with found objects, and an old linen curtain has been cleverly turned into a tablecloth. A bench provides seating along one wall.

In this 1850s period house, the dining area positively encourages creativity. The chimney breast is decorated with cut-out alphabet letters in different colours and materials. Books on shelves are left open to pages that inspire and amuse. The flower vase is an old ghee tin from India to which a handle has been added, while the table and chairs are Danish.

*An antique French door set on decorative legs
makes an elegant yet hardy dining table.
A glazed partition keeps cooking and eating
areas defined yet connected, whereas a smaller,
more informal table is set in the kitchen area
for homework, snacks and household office
use. Following pages: The table and chairs are
an Eero Saarinen design. To make the Harry
Potter picture, see page 68.*

homework Up to a certain age, homework is a communal activity, or at least one for which you're needed for reference, food supplies, reassurance, and to listen to a certain amount of complaining. Younger children like help at hand so they don't feel isolated or unsure. Letting them work in the kitchen makes learning a natural activity, and children don't feel banished to a separate area.

How do we help our children *celebrate* while also instilling a sense of
deeper VALUES? If we are anxious about preparations, how do we show
them it's not all about cake and presents? There is nothing wrong with
trying to make your children's birthday parties *special*, but do yourself
a favour – try to have FUN. Parties can be fraught and exhausting but
they can also make wonderful lasting *memories*. Celebrations are
where TRADITIONS are passed down: what we eat, what we wear, how we
decorate, the songs we sing. Mostly we learn to gather loved ones around
us and rejoice in our good fortune, not a bad tradition in itself.

celebrate one fine day

BIRTHDAY GIRL

Emotions can run high on even the most celebratory of occasions • There are bound to be expectations and disappointments, and to avoid tearful tantrums it is important to keep in mind that it is her day • To make the birthday girl feel special, ensure she feels involved by letting her choose the guests, help write the invitations and decorate the cake • Letting her wear a favourite outfit – or pair of fairy wings – could be enough to stave off the dramatic (and traditional) storming off to the bedroom.

BIRTHDAY CAKE

There are a million kinds of birthday cakes to make, and letting siblings help is a great way for them to show their appreciation for the birthday boy/girl • If you're short on time but still want a personal touch, buy a plain iced cake and add your own decorative sweets and trimmings • Use stencils and tube icing to decorate a whole cake or individual fairy cakes • If you're using edible decorations, be sure there is enough to include with each slice you serve out or there could be trouble.

party

PIRATES AND FAIRIES

It's always fun to have a theme to a party • Kids love to dress up, the sillier the better • Pirates: 'Message-in-a-bottle' invitations, 'treasure hunt' with maps, costume jewellery for treasure, keep extra eye patches on hand • Fairies: Lots of glitter, plastic and paper flowers and bubbles • Superheroes: Children come dressed as their favourite action figure and take turns performing amazing feats • Pyjamas: Guests are invited to party in their pyjamas, sleep over and drink hot chocolate with marshmallows!

PARTY BAGS

Parties should be about fun, but with the cost of the average party bag running anywhere from £5 to £25 (and I am sure there are some who will go even further) it seems we need to take a giant step back • A few sweets and a quirky little token should be all you need • As with anything, personal touches outshine expenditure every time • Customize labels and bags, a pirate invitation written on a paper eye patch, or another with fairy wings • Use coloured cellophane finished off with a ribbon or feathers.

PLAN AHEAD

Involve your child in preparations • Check that your child's best friend is free • Send out invitations one month in advance • Enjoy preparing food and decorations with your child • Buy blank cards in bulk and let your child make their own invitations • Know that this is a day for E-numbers • Give your child a disposable camera to capture their memories of the day • Two hours is plenty • Keep your sanity and enjoy!

entertain Adults need to have fun, too. It's important for parents to feel they have time for each other and for their friends, and it is essential for children to know that parents will do this. Don't feel guilty about putting children to bed before guests arrive, or allowing little ones only a quick hello before being tucked in. It is not harsh to say that friends coming for dinner would rather enjoy adult conversation than feel obliged to amuse little cherubs, no matter how enchanting.

Toys have been neatly tucked away and a clean-lined modern dining space is set for a lovely evening meal with guests. The table is a design by Voon Wong (based on a design by Monica Armani), the chairs are by B&B Italia and the chandelier is by Tord Boontje for Swarovski. Previous pages: Celebratory treats for the birthday girl include cakes from Konditor & Cook and sparkly flowers from Jane Packer.

nest

Cuddle up, read, bathe, stretch out and close your eyes. Can there ever be a place in your home that's too comfortable? It is instinctive to want to arrange our surroundings with the same care and order that a bird uses to make a safe bed for its mate and offspring, so thinking of the home as a nest isn't new. It's simply that we have become hyper-aware of almost all of our choices within the home.

With so much media attention aimed at interior design, we can hardly change a light bulb without wondering what it says about us. But nesting is personal. It's about how your home helps you achieve precious moments of relaxation, through the feel of soft bedding against your skin, the perfect lamp for curling up and reading in your much-loved chair, and bathing in your deep bath. When we consider the importance of rest and relaxation to our wellbeing, the value of building a calming environment that we are happy to come home to should not be underestimated. It might seem a bit frivolous to talk about good quality bedding and furnishings, but not when that quality is translated as something that helps us to unwind, sleep and refresh. While there are no hard and fast rules about creating spaces that are relaxing, there are certain approaches that make a good deal of sense. Often all that is required is a little time spent thinking about what could be changed and some small adjustments made using the resources to hand. You might decide to dispose of that chest of drawers that the children could never quite work properly, or find a place for a treasured quilt. Nesting is also about making time for rituals that induce calm and sleep. For adults this means the spaces where we unwind after dinner with a book, a drink, a conversation, a long bath. It's about attending to our own wellbeing so that we can be there for our families. Rooms that are restful and beautiful are more than practical or visually appealing, they inspire feelings of comfort, security and even delight, feelings that nurture rest, which is essential to a healthy mind, body and family.

rest

While there has been much research linking behavioural problems with lack of sleep, one only need witness one's own child after a bad night to know how vital it is that school-age children get their recommended ten hours of sleep. Regular routines of sleeping and waking in an environment designed to induce calm and comfort are necessary to help them achieve an adequate amount of dream time. Equally important is having parents who have taken the time to recuperate and rest, to feel able to cope with energetic, engaging and sometimes tired and irritable children.

sleep No matter which heavenly corner of the world we might be in, at some point we long to sleep in our own bed. One-third of our lives are spent sleeping, add to this the time we spend in bed reading, working, daydreaming, playing, just being, and you begin to sense just how significant this piece of furniture is to your home and to your life. More and more of us are losing sleep due to stress, yet only a few of us will invest in a good mattress. How strange that we will freely splash out on televisions, computers, cars, and indeed grand headboards, and yet think nothing of sleeping on a 'make-do' bed. This is the place where you start and end your day. It should be something to look forward to.

The vintage style of a customized blanket and pillowcase complement a painted antique bed frame in this boy's room. The bedding has been hand-stitched by Shirley McLauchlan with a cowboy motif and words from a favourite story, as well as lists of the boy's favourite foods. His footprints on canvas hang alongside the letters of his name and another special artwork. The western theme is played out further with cowboy curtains from Cath Kidston and a faux cowhide rug.

That night, and for many nights
after, the *Velveteen Rabbit* slept
in the Boy's bed.

Soon, he grew to like it, for the
Boy made nice tunnels for him
under the bedclothes that he
said were like the burrows the
real rabbits lived in.

When the Boy dropped off to
sleep, the Rabbit would snuggle
close *all night long*.

MARGERY WILLIAMS, *The Velveteen Rabbit*

A child's room can be minimal and fun. The acetate wall decoration by Mimi Lou adds character without too much fuss. The spare look of the bed frame made from recycled scaffolding poles is livened up with a vintage trunk, toys and vibrant colour on the rug and walls.

You'll never know which thing will become the *best-loved,* can't-do-without, the night-time necessity. It might be a hand-stitched hand-me-down, a bright new *soft* toy, or a well-used blanket. Whatever they choose, it will mean *security* to your children and bring a sense of personal belonging and wellbeing. And you'll end up *treasuring* it almost as much as they do.

comfort favourite things

treasure A child's bedroom is their own personal world. It's where they keep their most prized possessions, either locked away in a special box or proudly on display. This is their base and their comfort zone. It is also where they prepare for the days ahead. From here they will set out to discover the world in all its richness. And this is where they return to for rest and reassurance, with stories to tell.

Inspire your child to a lifetime of globetrotting with this atlas wallpaper from Urchin, a good way to remember family and friends in far-off places. The world in this boy's room is at his fingertips, alongside a cozy sleigh bed and Eames rocker. Previous page: Hand-knitted elephant by Sam McKechnie for The Magpie & The Wardrobe.

The dolls are the creation of Sam McKechnie for the The Magpie & The Wardrobe and are hand-painted, dressed in fabrics from antique ballgowns and decorated with vintage flowers and trimmings. An antique mirror frame finishes the tableau. Opposite: Old-fashioned and feminine, this is definitely a room for a little girl. The floral wallpaper, hand-made quilt and painted furniture all have a pretty, retro style, and a vintage party dress is just too beautiful to hide away.

COLLAGE

Covering an entire wall in a collage of pages from fashion or music magazines is a fun way to decorate a room, especially for the changing tastes of older children and teenagers. Use paste and a water-based lacquer to create a unique collection of images.

MAKING SPACES FUN

It's not just a question of paint or wallpaper, particularly with children's rooms. A soft tone of paint can be the backdrop for innovative treatments such as lettering, acetate silhouettes, artwork, blackboard paint or wallpaper, like this from Graham & Brown, that is actually an array of small empty frames just waiting for your artists-in-waiting to add their own touches. You probably don't want a riot of children's work all over the room, but in significant spaces it can be a way to add colour, fun and your child's own personality.

wall

LETTERLAND

Paint doesn't just add colour. Blackboard paint can make a wall into an easel, or it can be painted onto a custom-sized piece of wood and attached to the wall. Use magnetic paint in the same way to create a space for arranging magnetic letters and cut-outs in an ever-changing display. Alternatively, cut out letters in different sizes and paint with bold colours, or cut them from magazines or wallpaper to get a variety of bright patterns.

MURAL

A softer option than posters, a mural painted onto a wall, such as this one by Flora Roberts (far left), adds character to a room. Be sure you find a professional equipped to make the most of the space. Or make your own with an image from a child's favourite story. Just ensure that the colour and scale of the finished piece are right for the room.

CREATE THE SPIRAL

Wall decorations such as this spiral can also be decorative learning tools, incorporating poems, number rules or animal facts in interesting ways • Cut a piece of string to the size you want the radius of the circle to be • Tie one end of the string to a pencil and the other end to a bobbin or cup • Place the bobbin in the centre and hold the pencil tip to the wall • Draw the spiral, unrolling the string as you go • When you are finished, your spiral should be centred and even.

order Children's rooms also need to have some semblance
of order for them to become calm, restful places in which
to sleep or relax. A tidy wardrobe helps children learn how
to care for their things. Let them have some say about what
goes where, and some practice folding and stacking. Give
them storage that is easy to get to and show them where
clothes, books and toys go so they can help with putting
things away. Precious clothes displayed on walls do more
than look lovely, they act as a reminder to dress your child
in their special outfits while they still fit.

*Here, a large armoire has been used to display clothes and the drawers beneath have
been used to store toys. Opposite: The boys' dress clothes deserve to be on display,
but are hung well away from the shelf below to avoid looking cluttered. Overleaf:
A party dress and shoes, such as these from Caramel Baby & Child, make a pretty
accent in a bedroom when not in use, and a parent's antique mirror and marble-
topped dressing table hold the all-important list of weekly activities.*

identity As children grow older, they will want their bedroom — their space — to say something about them. Let them express their own personalities with a little gentle guidance and encouragement. Whether it's their own handiwork, the latest fashion magazines, or their carefully honed collection of toys or objects, you can help teenagers to show them off and enhance what they've chosen with a few added touches.

A teen's bedroom is bursting with expression. The needlepoint headboard is designed by Paul Smith for The Rug Company. Opposite: The wall is covered in pages from fashion and style magazines, applied with wallpaper glue and then varnished. The table is an Eileen Gray design, while the boldly patterned rug by Committee for The Rug Company adds to the modern feel.

A hand-knitted wool quilt, lively prints and patterns on the rug and furnishings spice up the plain painted walls, while a model airplane is best displayed in the air. The wall-hanging of a train is a needlepoint by Paul Smith for The Rug Company. Opposite: A collection of storybooks, toys, photographs and other keepsakes makes a unique and colourful display.

twos By the time we reach adulthood, most of us can't imagine how we ever shared a room. But most children love it. If a room is large enough for two beds, each child can have their own separate space or a spare for friends sleeping over – the perfect set-up for late-night giggling and whispered confidences.

The double sleigh beds with their generous tented fabric hangings have a fairytale feel. A high shelf above the door runs the full distance of the room, providing lots of out-of-the-way storage, while the mantelpiece is given a fairytale touch with a trompe l'oeil wall painting. The pair of Georgian-style doll's houses are painted wood.

The mesh wardrobe makes choosing clothes and toys easier for a child, and so encourages independence. The curved shelf is modern, easy to access and has smaller display shelves so that books and objects don't constantly collide. Opposite: Antique beds are given a contemporary feel covered in vibrant red linen fabric. The floor is polished concrete.

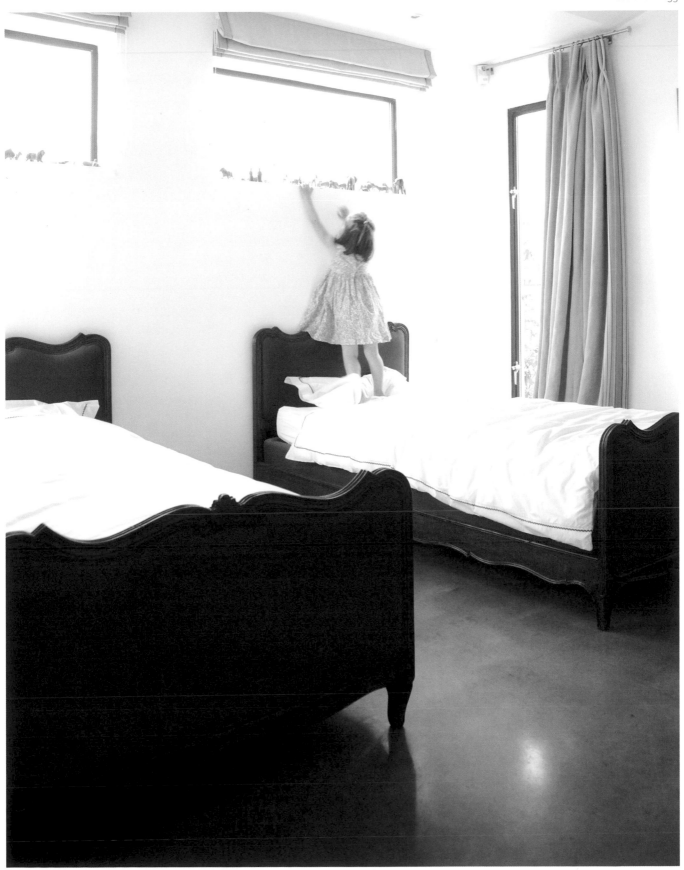

bunks Children adore bunk beds, the close proximity to the other sleeper and the cozy spaces. If it's siblings doubling up, then bunks make great space-savers and give more of the room over to train tracks, tea parties and battles, real or imagined.

This built-in bunk bed offers opportunities for storage and personal space. The lower bunk has storage hidden at one end. Shelves at each level provide space for each child's books and precious objects. Modern artworks and South African carved wood sculptures on display inspire creative young minds. The ladder rails are striped with coloured adhesive to match the bedding. Storage bowls by Créa Créa, diptych of fish by Susi Kramer, Polaroids by Peter Beard, fish painting by Mario Barzagli.

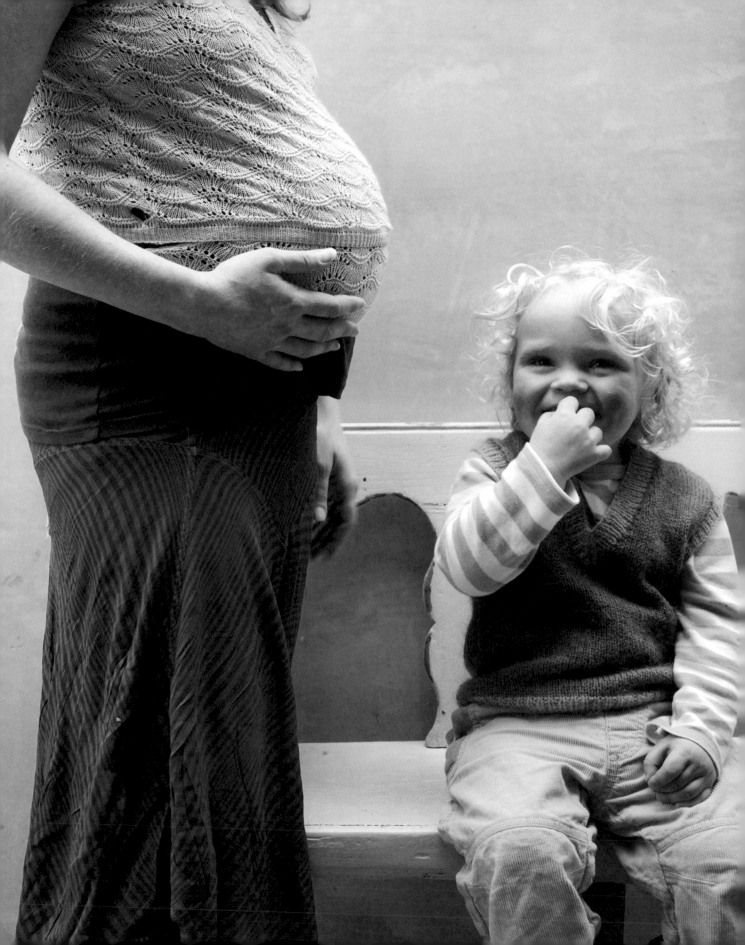

Love is what we want our *family* home to represent, a place where our children feel *cared* for and APPRECIATED, **nourished** and **nurtured**. Children build a *sense* of themselves and their *worth* through the family and how they are loved within it. If we are lucky enough we will have the *closeness* of grandparents, aunts, uncles, cousins to make us feel connected to others.

love

the essence of home

adapt Bouncers, walkers and swings may be vital but are only needed for a brief few months, so circulate. Cribs that have been used by friends or family are even better for the happy babies they have already held – just add a new mattress. With a newborn in the house, conversation often turns to the topic of sleep. Once you hit on a method or place that gets baby to sleep well, it will be like discovering the secrets of alchemy. If it happens to be your grand-mother's four-poster that does it, you'll be tempted to carry it around with you or never leave home. How lucky if the answer happens to be a portable rocker made with recycled cardboard.

An improvised nursery has been created on a large landing. The louvred shade can be closed to block the light from other rooms in the evening. Another nursery corner where a cot slides in next to a wardrobe to take up less of the shared space. Opposite: A cardboard cradle by Green Lullaby is compact, sturdy and portable.

Kitting out a whole nursery in the latest gear is tempting, but don't be afraid to improvise. It's what you do in the room that counts. This rocker is a classic design by Charles Eames. Opposite: The dining room converts to a baby's sleeping area with a fold-down changing table from Owo, sliding walls (one hiding ample storage, the other leading to the main living room), and a cot by Stokke that can be wheeled in and out. The dining table, too, is expandable.

precious It is great fun to decorate for children. We can indulge both their quirky tastes and some of our own. Vintage and modern, bold and delicate, mixing styles is not a crime. In fact, it's an opportunity to show more of your own personality and to give your child an inspiring start in life. Babies especially respond to light and to objects hanging in their view, so choose these with particular care.

An antique metalwork crib by Bonton, pretty wallpaper by Emilie Bazus, a softly glowing lamp and personal mementoes make for a very welcoming space. Textured cushions randomly placed on a miniature mattress make for a safe and comfortable play area. Creative wall pegs, including this design by Charles Eames opposite, and hooks always come in handy.

Worn by the *fairytale* hero, the colour of UNICORNS, the wizard's *beard* and the snowy forest. From the earliest fairy tales, white holds special significance in children's stories: SNOW White's beautiful PALE skin drives the queen to murderous jealousy, while the Snow Queen turns to white a cold, barren landscape. It is the talking *White Rabbit* who leads **Alice in Wonderland**, and the white UNICORN who is always a symbol of elusive *magic*.

white

purity of childhood

LINEN

White cotton maintains its look and feel even when washed at higher temperatures and bleached to get rid of stains • Colour can be added in other bedroom fabrics such as duvet covers, curtains and cushions • Wash bed sheets every five days • Use a top sheet and wash duvet cover every three weeks • As comforting as they are, feather-filled duvets are repositories for all sorts of human detritus and microbes and should be cleaned every six months • Unwashed duvets can aggravate skin conditions and asthmatic complaints.

CHOOSING A MATTRESS

When trying a new mattress, lie down and slide your hand under the small of your back • If you have to struggle to wedge your hand in, the mattress is too soft; if there is a hollow, the mattress is probably too hard • Go for a natural-fibre filling that can absorb body moisture • A water-resistant mattress topper is a worthwhile investment that will soften the mattress slightly and protect the valuable mattress underneath.

bed

QUIET TIME

Designate areas in the home where no television, radio or computer games are allowed • Give your children quiet time at least once a week when they can read, sit quietly, paint, draw, sew, play with (non-electronic) toys • Let them see you spending time quietly reading or sitting • Make quiet areas calmer with soft colours and lighting • Give children just a few objects to choose from that you know they enjoy • Try to encourage them to play independently • Keep a list of activities children are allowed to do during quiet time.

SLEEP

How much? It is recommended that newborns sleep sixteen to eighteen hours a day, toddlers have twelve to fourteen hours, school-age children get ten hours per night and adults between seven and eight, although recent studies suggest nine hours is better. The point is lack of sleep can produce all sorts of negative effects in adults and children. It is rare to meet the healthy child or adult who sleeps too much. It has even been suggested that many children diagnosed with ADHD also suffer from too little sleep.

BABIES

Put babies in sleeping blankets so they won't pull them off and give themselves a chill in the night, which might wake them and you • Be sure to put babies to sleep on their backs with their feet touching the end of the bed so they can't wriggle down under blanket • Never use down duvets for babies • Use breathable cotton and flannelette blankets, layered if needed, for warmth • Keep a lamp with a low-wattage bulb in the room or install dimmers for the least disturbance during night-time nappy changes.

me Parents need to be allowed their own rituals for relaxing. Children's needs may be considered in every other room in the house, but your bedroom should be a guilt-free zone designed to indulge your desires. Surround yourself with the things that make you feel good and bring comfort and a bit of luxury to your daily routine. Invest in a magnificent bed dressed in layers of linen and cashmere, oversized bedside tables and lamps and favourite books. Add little touches to seduces the senses with scented candles, fresh flowers and plants, soothing music and, if space permits, a comfy armchair in which to curl up and relax. Do whatever it takes to feel cared for and cherished, and do it with abandon.

An open-plan house still allows for parental privacy. The partition wall lets light flow through yet maintains a separate space for adults. The velvet-covered stools and padded headboard by Bruno Triplet, lamps by Ochre and zebra rug bespeak a grown-up sense of luxury. Swan chairs by Arne Jacobsen are pulled up to the modernized fireplace.

A parent's retreat in the upstairs space of a converted church features a neoclassical-style, mahogany-veneered bed set beneath a large circular window, which brings natural light into the space but still allows for some privacy. The children's portraits are by Claerwen James.

revive

We all enjoy the sensation of a refreshing shower or a warm bath. Children especially love water, even if they sometimes balk at the idea of getting clean. The most fretful babies can usually be calmed by a warm bath. They say it has something to do with being suspended in the womb, but we all feel comforted and relaxed when we're immersed in water. Children love the splash and flow, the floating and swirling. We love seeing them clean and contented. There's nothing like the elemental purity of water to bring us back to life.

routine It's hard to overstate the importance of routine in a child's daily life. Being able to predict what things will happen next helps them to feel secure. One of the most important routines that you will practice with your child involves the things you do at bedtime. A warm bath is an easy way to make a child feel settled physically and mentally in preparation for a truly restful sleep. It's also a good time for one-to-one attention.

Children don't need huge bathtubs to enjoy a good splash and soak. Here, a miniature roll-top bath by C.P. Hart has been fitted in the smallest of spaces, saving water and time. An accessible basin for teeth-brushing is essential. Previous pages: An open shower area is ideal for children who have trouble keeping water in control. Non-slip tile is a must on the floor.

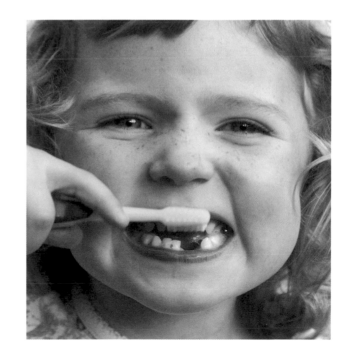

simple Whoever invented the plastic baby bath either had strong hired help or a very robust spine. In the days before kitchen and bathroom sinks became the victims of style, they were the most logical and handy places to wash babies. Few things are more precarious than trying to hold a slippery infant with one hand, while soaping and scrubbing with the other. Give yourself and your back a break. If you've got a lovely large basin, here's another reason to enjoy it.

scent Smell is a powerful sense. From an early age, babies are able to distinguish their own mother's scent from another's. We can all be transported back to a place in our memory just by the whiff of something familiar. We can make the most of the power of scent by choosing revitalizing, refreshing or relaxing fragrances for the bath, the bedroom and throughout the home. Essential oils are a good way to add fragrance, whether in a diffuser or dabbed on a cloth.

Opposite: The freestanding antique metal bath promises precious moments of relaxation and retreat. Placed below the crystal chandelier and silver-framed Venetian mirror, it is the picture of pure indulgence. This is a space for adult alone time. The rug is a traditional Moroccan wedding blanket.

Home is a place for HEALING physical and emotional wounds. We comfort and *soothe* our loved ones in many ways; we listen to their *woes* and try to reassure them. We tend to the minor bugs and hurts with *TRUSTED* family remedies and a *well*-stocked medicine cabinet with candy-coloured plasters included.

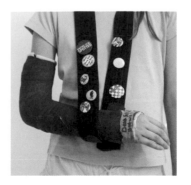

heal

wellbeing in our home

TEXTURE

There is nothing so soft as a baby's skin, but there are a wealth of fabrics with a variety of textures that are also a pleasure to feel • Softer materials are most appealing in the bedroom where they're more likely to be used next to bare skin • Mix velvets, satins, voiles and other soft fabrics to create an array of pleasurable sensations • In the bathroom, good-quality cotton bath towels will maintain their softness and absorbency and are a joy to snuggle up in after stepping from the bath.

BABY MASSAGE

As adults we are well aware of the benefits of deep massage, and we now know that babies, too, can benefit from similar methods • Massage has been shown to have a calming effect on even very new babies • It slows the heart rate, aids sleep and facilitates early infant communication, and may also help relieve nasal congestion, gas and digestive problems • Most importantly, through eye contact and physical closeness, it helps to build trust and enhance the bond between parent and child.

touch

soothe

THE SCENT OF HOME

One of the first things people will notice on entering your home is the welcoming scent that greets them • Let the scents in your home create a fragrant calendar • For spring, use the elegant and fresh smells of honeysuckle, hyacinth and narcissus • Summer is all about stronger scents like basil, fig and jasmine • For autumn, try a woody note like quince • Cinnamon is a scent redolent of winter, and as the nights draw in, create a festive atmosphere by making your own pomander and studding an orange with cloves.

WELLBEING

Essential oils can be used in a number of ways: in massage, in the bath, or dabbed on a hanky • Chamomile and lavender aid sleep and are thought to have a cooling effect in the case of fever, as does peppermint • Try geranium and bergamot for anxious adults and chamomile and geranium for fretful babies • Tea tree and lavender are recommended for clearing stuffy noses, and cinnamon, lavender and thyme for coughs • To cheer you on a tough day, try a little lemon or bergamot.

retreat

Everyone needs quiet time, even active young adults. An endless round of sports, music lessons and art classes might seem like the best way to realize a child's potential, but most experts agree that too much pushing and planning can make children agitated and unable to wind down. A constant series of activities can also inhibit sleep and stifle creativity and the development of independence. Children need time to do nothing, to let their minds rest or run without interference or limits. Spaces where this can happen are essential in the home. Yes, children need to be engaged in learning and developing, but they also need to learn to slow down, to stop, think, imagine and shut off.

read Learning to read is considered one of a child's most significant achievements, and it can be made a great deal easier if children get into the habit of sitting down with a book early on. As parents read to their children, they are sharing the pleasure of books together, teaching them how books work, how words go with pictures, and describing actions and scenes. As children look and listen, they use their imagination and their own natural curiosity to ask questions about the stories. Most importantly, they become comfortable with books and excited about being able to read for themselves. Unlike any computer game, television programme or film, books open up a child's imagination and creativity far beyond what is in front of them.

The nursery shelves held **books** galore!

Books cluttered up the nursery floor!

And in the bedroom, by the bed,

More **books** were waiting to be read!

Such wondrous, fine, fantastic tales

Of dragons, gypsies, queens and whales

And treasure isles, and distant shores

Where smugglers rowed with muffled oars,

And pirates wearing purple pants,

And sailing ships and elephants…

ROALD DAHL, *Charlie and the Chocolate Factory*

The rocking horse is a universal symbol of a children's play area. Here, this lovingly repaired family heirloom watches over a quiet corner where an oversized sheepskin beanbag beckons near shelves of storybooks. Opposite: A comfortable, well-lighted space, ideal for curling up with a story in leather chairs by M Pauw. Previous page: Both the bubble chair by Eero Aarnio and the rocking chair by Alexander Taylor in front of a mural by Flora Roberts provide cozy places for reading. Page 185: Portrait by Matthew Usmar Lauder, cashmere throw by Oyuna, table by David Gill.

pause We all need time to stop and stare. Without it we become hurried, anxious, unfocused. In a world of constant and sometimes overwhelming stimulation, it is more important than ever to have quiet time out. In religious societies, time is set apart for prayer and reflection. It is not a small gift to teach your children to value time for relaxed thought and contemplation.

bare

The chance to be free and independent, to feel the sun on your skin, jump in puddles, catch snowflakes on your tongue or simply enjoy the wonder of the clouds floating by, these are the priceless pleasures of being outdoors. As children we can doubtless recall spending many hours outdoors unsupervised. We had fewer television channels or computer games, and yet our world felt larger.

Today with media bombarding us from every corner of the globe, we feel a heightened sense of anxiety and cling to our children tightly. We are reluctant to let them walk to school, play in the park or even get their hands dirty, lest they catch some incurable rare disease. It is no wonder then that our children are not as fit as they should be and that cases of childhood obesity are on the rise. How do we break this cycle whilst still being mindful of the world around us? Children should be allowed and encouraged to get outdoors as much as possible, to run about, swing, climb, shout and laugh louder. There's nothing like stepping outside to calm a tantrum or a heated situation. Perhaps it is the need to expend physical energy that causes the tantrum in the first place, and simply being outdoors allows a child to let off steam and ward off an outburst even before it has begun. If we accept that we no longer feel safe letting our children wander the streets unsupervised, why not use this to our advantage by walking alongside them of an evening? Not only does this result in precious time together, it allows us the fresh air and exercise needed in maintaining a healthy mind and body. Outside is where we truly feel connected to the natural world. Worms in the soil, a ladybird on an arm, a spider in its web, all are fascinating to children. Looking at nature together in the garden is the best way to help them learn about their environment and how to nurture and care for it. Let them dig and explore, feel the soil between their fingers, grass on their bare feet, mud everywhere. You can always wash them. In fact, they'd probably like nothing better than a good old drenching fight afterwards.

free

No matter how open or grand your living space, there is nothing quite like the all-out, open-air freedom of being outdoors. Children especially need room to let go, to leave the confined atmosphere of household order and knock about on their own, whether playing games together or just having a lazy wander in the grass. It's great if you want to join them in a round of hopscotch or cricket, but it's just as important for them to be left to get on with their own imaginations and freestyle fun.

active Children need physical exercise. There is simply no substitute. Developing muscles, bones and minds benefit from regular physical activity. It also helps children unwind mentally and emotionally, as it does adults, and they will sleep better at night if they have exerted themselves during the day. Naturally children are much more likely to get into games and exercise if they're encouraged to get outdoors as often as possible.

You need space for wheeled vehicles, but a small patch of grass or deck will do for a little cricket or raquet games. Use a smaller, softer ball if your space is very limited. Opposite: A retro model Mercedes-Benz is great for pedalling round the garden and later for passing on to the next generation of children.

vent For anxiety, frustration, nervous energy or just plain excitement, nothing beats a good run, jump, skip, sing or dance round the garden or park. Playing outdoors needn't be about structured activities, sometimes children just need to let off a little steam. Though they may be reluctant to pry themselves away from the television, computer or Playstation, they almost always find a way to let loose once they're through the door.

Trampolines are great exercise tools. Sunk in the ground is best, as children do not have so far to fall. Higher trampolines can be surrounded with soft materials for safe landings. Some models are equipped with a netted surround to keep children from missing their target.

ACTIVITY

Apart from having improved muscle development and co-ordination, children who are physically fit perform better academically • Children should have forty minutes to an hour of physical activity every day • Younger children who get an average of forty minutes vigorous daily activity develop greater bone density, resulting in stronger, healthier bones • Try limiting computer and television time, even at the risk of much moaning and groaning, so that children are encouraged to get outdoors and be active.

GAMES

Even a small garden can accommodate a game of hopscotch, skipping ropes, badminton and shuttlecock (kids adore this even without a net), balls for catching, kicking and throwing (use softer balls to avoid damage to plants and pots), table tennis and other paddle games • An inflated beach ball makes a brilliant, and safe, volleyball • Some of the most enduring games require no extra gear at all, from playground favourite 'It', to hide-and-seek, to dancing in a ring to the accompaniment of songs, rhymes and clapping.

fit

fun

PASS IT ON

The simplest activities can be the most fun • Grandmothers over the centries have shared the secrets of making a daisy chain, sewing a straight seam, coaxing a flower from a plant, baking the perfect cake • Moments like these are about more than learning a new skill, they are about shared time and creating precious memories that we treasure and pass on to the next generation of little girls.

BUBBLES

Children everywhere are enchanted by bubbles • The glistening, delicate wonder of soap and water is such a simple way to make a few magical moments with your child • Even toddlers can learn to blow through a wand and you only need a small patio space to create a bubble-filled wonderland • Make your own with ½ cup washing-up liquid to 5 cups water • If the mixture is too thick add a touch more water, if too thin add a bit more soap • Save up old bubble wands or use a kitchen whisk or plastic spoon with a hole.

escape We adults think we know what it's like to need time off from work and household concerns, but sometimes children need a break, too. As wonderful as it is for them to be able to run wild, it is also important for them to just have time to sit and think and wonder, and a place where they can be left alone to their own devices. A cool patch under the trees is just the place for drifting and daydreaming. An outdoor mind is a wandering, imaginative mind, unhindered by rules and expectations, free to dream.

Garden ponds are delightful places for children to study nature up close. Choose a range of plants that encourage your pond's wildlife to flourish. Always ensure that a garden pond is fitted properly with a safety grate just below the surface. This will allow plants to grow and even fish to swim through while protecting small children from falling under water.

drench Whether it's standing in
a sudden rain shower, jumping in
puddles, being blasted by a water
pistol or diving into a deep blue pool,
there is something about water play
that makes youngsters squeal with
delight. It is an excitement we seem
to lose as we grow older, but which
we can all recover when we see
children revelling in the sheer
wonder of water. Splashing about
is especially fun when there's a little
naughtiness involved, like squirting
your sister when she's not looking!

*An indoor/outdoor spa area features an open shower
and small lap pool. Patterned tiles and large antique
jars complement the Mediterranean style.*

Swimming is fantastic *body*-strengthening exercise for all children, even for those who aren't the most athletic. Children who might feel awkward on the playing field often feel *liberated* in the water. Learning how to swim is a fundamental RITE OF PASSAGE, like riding your first bike, and it is vital for water safety. Parents who swim with their children from an early age develop a special BOND with them, and get to enjoy water fights all over again.

splash

dive right in

connect

We can all benefit from feeling closer to nature, feel the breeze on our skin, watch it move through the trees and clouds above. Children who learn about their environment, about the lifecycles of plants and animals and the effect of human beings on the planet we all share, develop a greater understanding of life and the delicate balance we must maintain. Teaching them about nature and their place in it gives them an important sense of connection to the wider world, as well as to what's going on under their feet.

nurture Nature is all around us, offering wonderful opportunities for everyone to enjoy and lend a helping hand. Looking after animals and plants gives children a sense of responsibility and achievement and helps them learn about lifecycles, about patience and the importance of caring for the world around them. Caring for nature also helps children understand the sources of the foods we eat and the importance of using our natural produce well and without waste.

Children should not only be allowed but *encouraged* to get their hands **dirty**, to hold a worm or a *spider* and see how it moves, to feel a ladybird crawl on their skin. They can hold a leaf in their hands and *trace* the veins and the holes where a caterpillar has had its lunch. We all learn by doing and it is far more meaningful to *touch* the EARTH, the leaves and roots of plants with your own hands, than to look at them from afar.

feel

flourish and blossom

SEEDS

Cress can be grown easily in a cup with only a wet paper towel. And you can eat it in days! • Sunflowers are very satisfying to watch, especially the giant variety, which will grow dramatically in good sunlight • Radishes are easy to grow and can be eaten within a month • Sweet peas love to be picked, as it only makes them grow more flowers • Marigolds planted in March or September can flower in ten weeks and the petals of the *officinalis* variety are edible • Nasturtium is another colourful flower that is tasty, too.

IN THE GARDEN

Digging, hoeing, planting seeds and watering are all jobs that children will love to help with • If you haven't got room for a garden plot, try growing little seedlings, pots of herbs or a giant sunflower with your child to experience the wonder of nature together • Go for lavender, rosemary, sage and hardy perennials • Children will love helping with some basic tools of their own • Bucket and spade (even a large spoon or fork will do) • Watering can • Colourful, rainproof rubber boots • Seed packets, bulbs, plants of their own choosing.

grow

BULBS

A fantastic way to celebrate the autumn season is to make a ritual of bulb planting, whether around the grassy edges of the lawn or in pots on the terrace. Make sure you plant them to full effect for their blooming season. Snowdrops generally crop up in very early spring followed by their more colourful cousins, the crocuses and tulips. Finally, the jolly range of yellows, golds and creams in the daffodils to herald the arrival of spring.

FRUITS AND FLOWERS

Wild strawberries are easy to grow indoors or out and children love the sweet, delicious fruit • Lavender is a colourful, aromatic plant that will bring a lively hum of bees into your garden • Bellflowers, or 'Canterbury Bells', bloom in blue, white or lavender and flower in the summer. A wonderfully child-friendly flowering plant • Children love pansies for their happy little faces and the colour they bring in winter and summer • Lambs' ears are lovable for their soft, furry leaves that resemble the woolly animals' own ears.

DIG IN

Soil is a wonderfully rich material when you actually get down to it • Full of nutrients, roots, rocks and found objects, it's also home to a fantastic array of crawling creatures • Some children won't want to get their hands dirty, others will want to drive toy trucks through, and then there are those who will find bliss in a puddle of mud • Keep some plastic containers on hand for temporary 'pets' such as beetles and caterpillars as there's nothing like watching the smallest friends of the earth close up.

seasons It's not just the turn of the clock that stirs us as time passes, it's also the changes of the earth. As we see the leaves going from green to yellow to brown, we note the chill settling in and feel connected to the natural cycle of things. In celebration of that connection we make the most of what's on offer throughout the year. Autumn is a time for gathering up the harvest and playing with conkers, jumping in leaves and planting spring bulbs. Winter is for drawing in and warming up together during frosty nights. In spring we are inspired by the appearance of the first buds and blossoms, and in summer we rush outdoors to feel the return of the sun and appreciate nature's bounty in full.

inside out

We all like being outdoors, while preserving some of the comforts of indoors. When a room is added on to a house, it is most often one that can be opened to the outdoors and makes moving in and out easy and comfortable. Children, too, love wandering in and out, as any parent trying to keep a floor clean will know. Outdoor rooms are gardens that are almost part of the house, grown-up spaces that are a little less precious than the rest of the home and a lot more relaxed, and children's spaces that are little hideouts, sometimes where adults are not allowed.

hideaway What child doesn't love to have a special
place to retreat from the adult world into their own?
What adult wouldn't love to have one, too? Treehouses,
playhouses, huts and tents give children a quiet space
to think and imagine, to bring their friends (real and
imaginary) for tea, cakes and pow-wows. You can build
your own with some spare parts and a little ingenuity
or buy one ready-made and save yourself the extra effort
(and potential embarrassment). Or make an easy version
with bed sheets and chairs (indoors or out) – crawling in
and out is half the fun.

*A mini version of a thatched cottage lets children play house, even down to the al
fresco table and chairs. Opposite: A tidy treehouse made-to-order with trimmed
willow branches fits right in with the greenery.*

outdoor rooms Some garden spaces are designed with ease of use in mind, so paving, benches and other seating make them civilized and comfortable. But spaces like utility rooms, conservatories, enclosed porches and greenhouses are invaluable for life with children, spaces where the muck and mess are more easily coped with, and where children are more free to move outdoors at will. These are great places for storing all the outdoor equipment, but make sure you leave room enough for lingering on rainy days and carrying the picnic goodies through.

An enclosed sun porch is used for storing everything from art supplies to toys. It's also a good place for a snack and all those activities that bring kids traipsing indoors and out. Previous pages: Children can jump directly from the treehouse into this small pool, which can be packed away when the weather turns cold.

A well-designed playhouse, complete with rustic desk and blackboard. Opposite: This landscaped urban garden features plenty of decking space and concrete steps that also function as seating below the lawn, which has been made level and well suited to ball games.

A courtyard garden is one of the most prized spaces in this modern house. With the openness and greenery of outside and the security of home, it makes an ideal place for relaxing.

al fresco The Italians invented the phrase, but that doesn't mean that eating outdoors is limited to warm Mediterranean climes. Spring and summer in most places bring enough good weather to draw us outside for the occasional lunch and dinner, or even cocktails under the stars amid the scents of night-blooming plants. The smallest patio or terrace, too often claimed as a storage area, should be left clear of clutter. Set out a few plants and keep collapsible chairs nearby so that you can grab the first chance at an outdoor supper or a quiet morning coffee.

A brick-paved patio area outside a country cottage makes an ideal spot for outdoor eating. Plants have been kept close to the walls to allow plenty of space for seating. The table and chairs are well weathered, but could be covered with a cloth and cushions to create a more formal setting.

Some things just taste better when eaten outdoors. Ice cream drips, lollies melt, crumbs drop, juice plops. Those things that would be indoor horrors make us smile and laugh. Taking TREATS outside is *relaxing* for everybody, and you don't always need a hot day to enjoy them. Faced with a crowd of eager faces, pile the snacks and drinks on a tray and lead them out to where mess doesn't matter. Then let them tuck in with *abandon*.

 eat with abandon

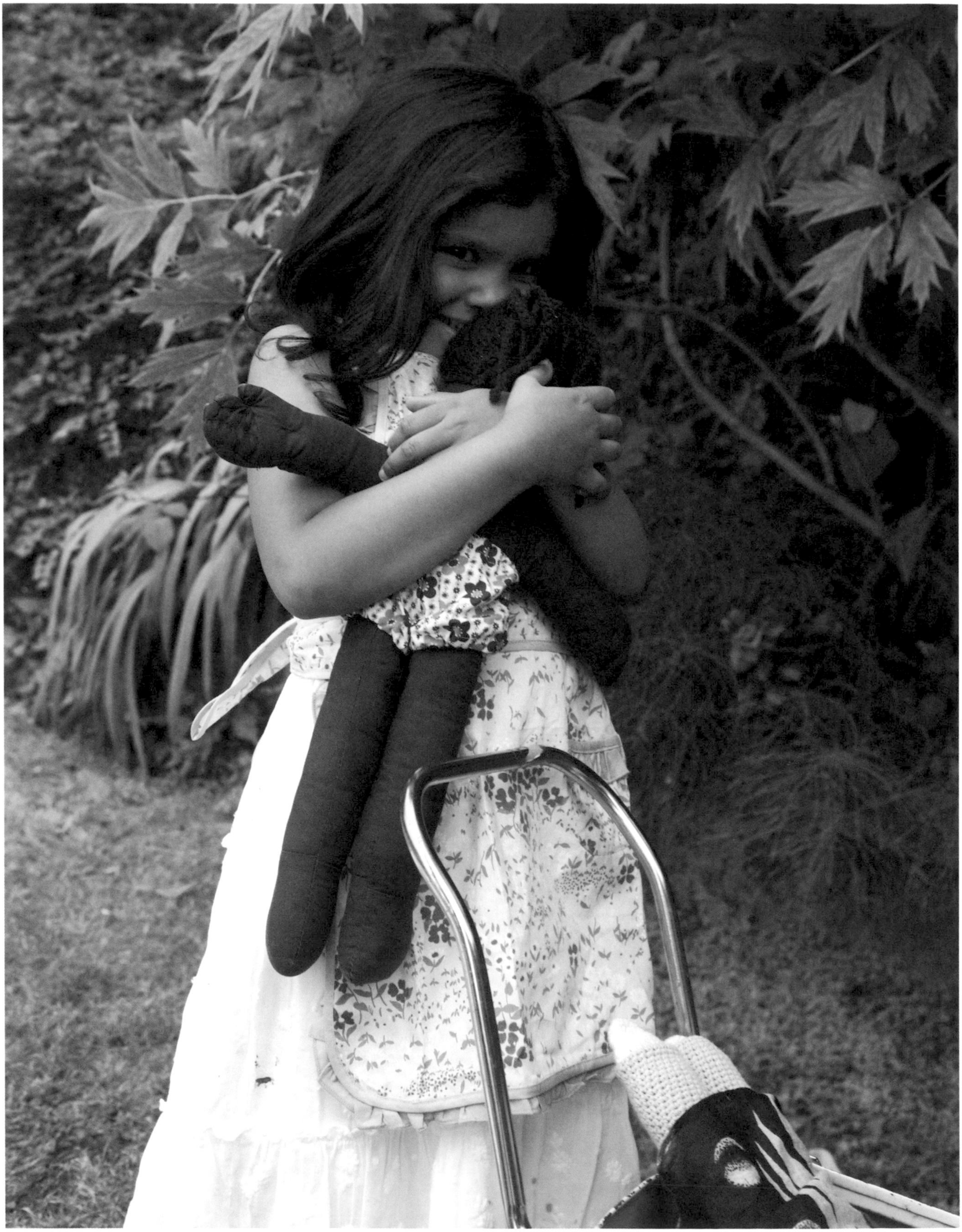

A children's picnic combines the fun of the outdoors with the joy of sharing treats. A colourful cloth from Enkla made from children's drawings makes the perfect picnic blanket. Bright plastic plates, trays and mugs are filled with party 'food' such as cakes, biscuits and a few healthy snacks. Opposite: Don't forget to invite a few other special friends. This pretty apron is from a women's cooperative in Africa.

Cold hands and a **warm** fire, roasted marshmallows and crackling chestnuts, candied apples and *hot* chocolate with CREAM, fireworks and fancy dress: who says the outdoors is best in summer weather? WRAPPING up in warmest, *woolliest* jumpers and stomping around in b**ig** boots is part of the *fun* of winter. And it's a wonderful kind of cold, when we really feel the frost in the air and we know that we'll soon be back *safely* in our own, wonderfully warm, comfortable home.

kindle

the joy of family

You are the bows from which
your **children** as living arrows
are sent forth.

<small>KAHLIL GIBRAN, *The Prophet*</small>

find

A directory of designers, manufacturers and shops whose products feature in this book. Numbers in brackets refer to page numbers.

ARCHITECTS, ARTISTS, DESIGNERS, STUDIOS AND INTERIORS

Blake House [12–13, 47, 58, 86–87, 110–11, 145, 168–69, 179, 188–89]
Available for location hire
1st Option Representation
64 Upper Walkway
West Yard, Camden Lock
London NW1 8AF
T +44 (0)20 7284 2345
E mail@1st-option.com
W www.1st-option.com

Tord Boontje [120, 121]
Designer
La Cour, Route de Graix
42220 Bourg-Argental
T +33 (0)477 396 604
E info@tordboontje.com
W www.tordboontje.com

Jonathan Clark Architects [160, 161]
Architects
34–35 Great Sutton Street
London EC1V 0DX
T +44 (0)20 7608 111
E jonathan@jonathanclarkarchitects.co.uk
W www.jonathanclarkarchitects.co.uk

Marianne Cotterill [34, 35]
Wallpaper designer
T +44 (0)20 8451 0895

Créa Créa [14–15, 154–55]
Designers; products available through Pylones
E webcontact@pylones.com
W www.pylones.com

The Curved House [236, 237]
Available for location hire
T +44 (0)020 8675 3269
E anjanadevoy@aol.com
W www.curvedhouse.com

Claerwen James [69, 170, 171, 252]
Artist
Flowers Central Gallery
21 Cork Street
London W1S 3LZ
T +44 (0)20 7439 7766
E central@flowerseast.com
W www.flowerseast.com

Ella Doran Design [26–27, 142]
Interior design
46 Cheshire Street
London E2 6EH
T +44 (0)20 7613 0782
E info@elladoran.co.uk
W www.elladoran.co.uk

Nell Johnson [24, 25, 68]
Artist
T +44 (0)7789 866262
E neris@rubyfilms.co.uk
W www.nelljohnson.co.uk

Matthew Usmar Lauder [185, 252]
Artist
E snake.eeemail@virgin.net
W www.matthewusmarlauder.com

Bruno Triplet [169]
Textile designer
23 Elystan Street
London SW3 3NT
T +44 (0)20 7823 9990
E sales@brunotriplet.com
W www.brunotriplet.com

Voon Wong Architects [74–75, 120, 121, 122–23, 154–55, 185, 235]
Architects
Unit 27, 1 Stannary Street
London SE11 4AD
T +44 (0)20 7587 0116
E info@voon-wong.com
W www.voon-wong.com

SHOPS

After Noah [61]
Furniture, lighting and toys
121 Upper Street
London N1 1QP
T +44 (0)20 7359 4281
E enquiries@afternoah.com
W www.afternoah.com

The Cross [56, 72–73, 80, 81, 130, 131]
Cult fashion and accessories boutique
141 Portland Road
London W11 4LR
T +44 (0)20 7727 6760

David Gill Gallery [185]
Furniture and artwork for the home
60 Fulham Road
London SW3 6HH
T +44 (0)20 7589 5946

Divertimenti [91]
Kitchen supplies and cookware
227–229 Brompton Road
London SW3 2EP
T+44 (0)20 7581 8065
E brompton@divertimenti.co.uk
33/34 Marylebone High Street
London W1U 4PT
T+44 (0)20 7935 0689
E marylebone@divertimenti.co.uk
W www.divertimenti.co.uk

Grand Illusions [105]
Home and garden accessories
41 Crown Road
St Margarets, Surrey TW1 3EJ
T +44 (0)20 8607 9446
37 High Street
Shaftesbury, Dorset SP7 8JE
E info@grandillusions.co.uk
W www.grandillusions.co.uk

M Pauw [189]
Leather chairs and sofas
Cooper House, 2 Michael Road
London SW6 2AD
T +44 (0)20 7731 4022

Ochre [169]
Furniture, lighting and bespoke chandeliers
27/31 Clerkenwell Close
London EC1R 0AT
T +44 (0)870 787 9242
E enquiries@ochre.net
462 Broome Street
New York, NY 10013
T +1 212 414 4332
E usenquiries@ochre.net
W www.ochre.net

Oyuna [185]
Cashmere for home, fashion and baby
35 Britannia Row
London N1 8QH
T +44 (0)870 066 7145
E info@oyunacashmere.com
W www.oyuna.com

Thorsten van Elten [5, 187]
Furniture, lighting, clothing, accessories
22 Warren Street
London W1T 5LU
T +44 (0)20 7388 8008
E info@thorstenvanelten.com
W www.thorstenvanelten.com

ONLINE SHOPS

Angelique [183]
Skincare for mother and baby
T +44 (0)20 8769 1258
E info@angelique.co.uk
W www.angelique.co.uk

The Magpie & The Wardrobe [102, 103, 135, 138, 139, 232, 233, 250]
Hand-made dolls, jewellery and 'fripperies'
T +44 (0)7770 961 362
E sam@magpiewardrobe.co.uk
W www.magpiewardrobe.co.uk

FURNITURE, BUILDING AND
INTERIOR SUPPLIES

B&B Italia [121]
Contemporary Italian design
W www.bebitalia.it

Boffi [106–7]
Kitchen and bathroom design
W www.boffi.com

Cappellini [42]
Modern furniture design
W www.cappellini.it

C.P. Hart [174]
Contemporary bathroom design
W www.cphart.co.uk

Dalsouple [106–7]
Rubber flooring
W www.dalsouple.com

Graham & Brown [140]
Designer wallpaper
W www.grahambrown.com

Ikea [19, 32–33]
Affordable Swedish design
W www.ikea.com

Owo [160, 248]
Online design store
W www.owo.it

Tanguy Rolin [19, 84–85, 158, 174]
Contemporary furniture and artwork
W www.tanguyrolin.co.uk

Stokke [160, 248]
Children's furniture and accessories
W www.stokke.com

Swarovski [120, 121]
Crystal lighting, jewellery and accessories
W www.swarovski.com

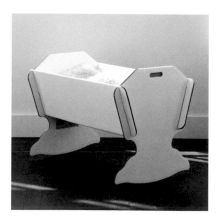

HOME ACCESSORIES

Bycamera [34, 35]
Photographs on canvas
P.O. Box 43823
London NW6 6XE
T +44 (0)20 8968 9889
W www.bycamera.co.uk

Cath Kidston [131]
English design for the home
W www.cathkidston.co.uk

Diptyque [178, 183]
Parisian fragrance company
W www.diptyqueparis.com

Jo Malone [145]
Fragrance for both body and home
W www.jomalone.co.uk

Jane Packer [116, 119]
Fresh, innovative floristry
32–34 New Cavendish Street
London W1G 8UE
T +44 (0)20 7935 2673
E flowershop@janepacker.com
407 East 59th Street
New York, NY 10022
T +1 212 754 1731
E flowerstore@janepacker.com
W www.jane-packer.co.uk

Maison de Vacances [44–45, 182, 183]
French interiors and lifestyle company
63–64 Galerie de Montpensier
Jardins du Palais Royal
75001 Paris
T +33 (0)1 47 03 99 74

E info@maisondevacances.com
W www.maisondevacances.com

Shirley McLauchlan [130, 131]
Hand-stitched bags, cushions and blankets
T +44 (0)1292 477 944
W www.skmclauchlan.co.uk

The Rug Company [14–15, 23, 32–33, 36–37, 54–55, 146, 147, 148, 251]
Designer and bespoke floor coverings
124 Holland Park Avenue
London W11 4UE
T +44 (0)20 7229 5148
E london@therugcompany.info
88 Wooster Street
New York, NY 10012
T +1 212 274 0444
E newyork@therugcompany.info
8202 Melrose Avenue
Los Angeles, CA 90046
T +1 323 653 0303
E la@therugcompany.info
W www.therugcompany.info

JUST FOR KIDS

Bonton [162–63]
Classic French furniture, fashion and accessories
82, rue de Grenelle
75007 Paris
T +33 (0)1 44 39 09 20
W www.bonton.fr

Caramel Baby & Child [14–15, 144]
Chic clothing and accessories
291 Brompton Road
London SW3 2DY
T +44 (0)20 7589 7001

E info@caramel-shop.co.uk
W www.caramel-shop.co.uk

Enkla [243]
Storage solutions and activity kits
21 Broad Street
Bath BA1 5LN
T +44 (0)1225 339789
E inspireme@enkla.co.uk
W www.enkla.co.uk

Green Lullaby [159, 252]
Recyclable furniture and accessories
T +972 (0)9 950 4094
E info@green-lullaby.com
W www.green-lullaby.com

The Lion & Unicorn Bookshop [186]
Books for kids
19 King Street
Richmond, Surrey TW9 1ND
T +44 (0)20 8940 0483
E services@lionunicornbooks.co.uk
W www.lionunicornbooks.co.uk

Urchin [136, 137, 140]
Ideas for parties, travel and games
T +44 (0)1672 518640
E help@urchin.co.uk
W www.urchin.co.uk

CHILDREN'S PARTIES

Cookie Crumbles [78, 80, 253]
Cooking activities for children
T +44 (0)845 601 4173
E carola@cookiecrumbles.net
W www.cookiecrumbles.net

Kasimira Party Organisers [115]
From birthday parties to corporate events
T +44 (0)20 7581 8313
E enquiries@kasimira.com
W www.kasimira.com

Konditor & Cook [116, 118]
Cakes and other baked goods
22 Cornwall Road
London SE1 8TW
T +44 (0)20 7261 0456
E cornwallroad@konditorandcook.com
W www.konditorandcook.com

Peggy Porschen Cakes [114]
Cakes for all occasions
32 Madison Studios
101 Amies Street
London SW11 2JW
T +44 (0)20 7738 1339
E info@peggyporschen.com
W www.peggyporschen.com

Penny Sweet Shop [101, 253]
Classic British sweets
2 Low Road
Norwich NR12 0DH
E questions@pennysweetshop.com
W www.pennysweetshop.com

The Vanilla Card Company [117]
Stationery made from children's artwork
Churwell Vale, Shaw Cross Business Park
Dewsbury, West Yorkshire WF12 7RD
T +44 (0)845 450 1878
E info@vanillacards.com
W www.thevanillacardcompany.co.uk

Online resources to aid and inspire, whether planning your child's birthday party or furnishing the baby's bedroom.

Angel Song
Imaginative children's furnishings
www.angelsong.net

Aram
Modern furniture classics
www.aram.co.uk

Bailey Flower Essences
Composite and single-flower essences
www.baileyessences.com

Born
All things organic
www.borndirect.co.uk

Bump To 3
For mother and baby
www.bumpto3.com

Birthday Party Express
Does it all, from ideas to balloons
www.birthdaypartyexpress.com

Cake Modern
Eclectically decorated cakes and biscuits
www.cakemodern.com

Calesta Kidstore
Lifestyle store with a Parisian design sensibility
www.calesta.fr

Carolyn MacKenzie
Original cake design
www.carolynmackenzie.co.uk

Celebrations: The Party People
Party decorations, supplies and novelties
www.celebrations-party.co.uk

Chick Shack
Furniture inspired by 18th century French and Swedish design
www.chickshack.net

The Conran Shop
More modern furniture classics
www.conran.com

Daisy & Tom
A magical shopping experience
www.daisyandtom.co.uk

Design Her Gals
Fun and interactive stationery designs
www.designhergals.com

Duffy London
Turn your child's artwork into a screen, a table, even wallpaper
www.duffylondon.com

Ear To Ear
The best gourmet popcorn ever
www.ear-to-ear.com

Egg and Spoon
1,001 things for babies
www.eggandspoon.com.au

Enchanted
Charming Manhattan toy store
www.enchanted-toys.com

First Way Forward
Hypnosis CDs to help conquer anxiety, thumb sucking, bedwetting, and more
www.firstwayforward.com

Genius Jones
Pre-eminent, high-design Miami store
www.geniusjones.com

Green Baby
Organic furniture, clothing and skincare
www.greenbaby.co.uk

Helios Homeopathic Pharmacy
Essential home kits for every alternative medicine cabinet
www.helios.co.uk

Kids Gallery
Nursery furniture and accessories
www.kidsgallery.fr

Lilliput Direct
Maternity wear and everything for baby
www.lilliputdirect.co.uk

Lionwitchwardrobe
Hand-crafted furniture for both children and adults
www.lionwitchwardrobe.co.uk

The Little White Company
Children's version of a favourite store
www.thewhitecompany.com

Magis Design
Children's furniture by leading designers
www.magisdesign.com

Modern Seed
Furniture, fashion and accessories with a modern edge
www.modernseed.com

Namemaker
Ribbon and wrapping paper printed with party details or personalized messages
www.namemaker.com

Netto Collection
New York furniture and accessories company
www.nettocollection.com

Ooba
Bassinets, rockers and accessories for babies
www.ooba.com

The Organic Pharmacy
Wellbeing through homeopathy and skincare
www.theorganicpharmacy.com

Party Directory
Crafts, games and music for parties
www.partydirectory4kids.co.uk

Petit Pan
French furniture and accessories for kids
www.petitpan.com

A Quarter Of
Nostalgic online sweetshop
www.aquarterof.co.uk

Rubadubdub
Personalized towelling products for baby
www.rubadubdub.co.nz

Sentou Raspail
Parisian furniture and accessories
www.sentou.fr

Serendipity
Vintage-inspired furniture for children
www.serendipity.fr

Their Nibs
Designer kids' clothes
www.theirnibs.com

Tots To Teens Furniture Barn
Furniture specialist for children of all ages
www.totstoteensfurniture.co.uk

Two Left Feet
Great for furniture, buggies, accessories
www.twoleftfeet.co.uk

Wigwam Kidz
An extensive collection of modern and classic furniture, delivered assembled
www.wigwamkidz.com

You Plus One
Massage and care for babies and expectant and new mothers
www.youplusone.co.uk

Thank you to all at Thames & Hudson for their invaluable advice and guidance; it is a privilege to work with such a great team. All my gratitude to Penny Wincer for capturing my thoughts and ideas so beautifully on camera, and to Alex Lewis for great styling and sense of humour. I have been fortunate enough to meet some extraordinary families, and I thank each and every one for welcoming me into their homes. Thank you to my parents for the valuable life lessons they have taught me and who, after fifty years together, prove what it is to love unconditionally, and to my six siblings, who I adore and admire in equal measure. Finally, a huge thank you to my dearest husband Bittu and children Milli and Manav for their boundless love and support and for making the space we share a place I can call home.

All photographs by Penny Wincer except for the following: Mimi Lou/Serendipity 2–3, 132, 251; Peter Strube/Maison de Vacances 44–45, 182 (all), 183 (middle); Alastair Merrill 78; F. Delafraye/Bonton 162–63.
Extract from *Charlie and the Chocolate Factory* by Roald Dahl, copyright text and illustrations © 1964, renewed 1992 by Roald Dahl Nominee Limited. Used by permission of Alfred A. Knopf, an imprint of Random House Children's Books, a division of Random House, Inc.
Special thanks to Ravenscourt Park Prep School, London and Allfarthing Primary School, Wandsworth.

Texts copyright © 2007 by Anita Kaushal
Photographs by Penny Wincer copyright © 2007 by Anita Kaushal

Published in the United States by Clarkson Potter/Publishers, an imprint of the Crown Publishing Group, a division of Random House, Inc., New York.
www.crownpublishing.com
www.clarksonpotter.com

Originally published in Great Britain by Thames & Hudson Ltd, London, in 2007.

Clarkson N. Potter is a trademark and Potter and colophon are registered trademarks of Random House, Inc.

Library of Congress Cataloging-in-Publication Data is available upon request.

ISBN 978-0-307-39445-3

Printed in China

10 9 8 7 6 5 4 3 2 1

First American Edition